CORE LIBRARY OF US STATES

ARIZONA

BY AUDREY HARRISON

CONTENT CONSULTANT
Alison Stoltman
Acting Director, Arizona Museum of Natural History

Core Library

An Imprint of Abdo Publishing
abdobooks.com

abdobooks.com

Published by Abdo Publishing, a division of ABDO, PO Box 398166, Minneapolis, Minnesota 55439.

Core Library™ is a trademark and logo of Abdo Publishing.

Printed in the United States of America, North Mankato, Minnesota.
052022
092022

THIS BOOK CONTAINS RECYCLED MATERIALS

Cover Photo: Shutterstock Images, map and icons; Red Line Editorial, capitol
Interior Photos: Johnny Adolphson/Shutterstock Images, 4–5; iStockphoto, 7, 18 (flag), 18 (bird), 18 (tree), 23, 43; Red Line Editorial, 9 (Arizona), 9 (USA); PhotoQuest/Archive Photos/Getty Images 10–11, 45; George H. H. Huey/Alamy, 12; Shutterstock Images, 14; Ken Canning/iStockphoto, 18 (flower); Minakryn Ruslan/iStockphoto, 18 (copper); Marisa Estivill/Shutterstock Images, 20–21; Jon Manjeot/Shutterstock Images, 25; Chuck Schug Photography/iStockphoto, 28–29; Jami Rae/iStockphoto, 30; Keeton Gale/Shutterstock Images, 33; Sean Pavone/iStockphoto, 34–35; Jamie Sue Photography/Shutterstock Images, 36; Stephanie LeMaire/Hemis/Alamy, 39

Editor: Katharine Hale
Series Designer: Joshua Olson

Library of Congress Control Number: 2021951402

Publisher's Cataloging-in-Publication Data

Names: Harrison, Audrey, author.
Title: Arizona / by Audrey Harrison
Description: Minneapolis, Minnesota : Abdo Publishing, 2023 | Series: Core library of US states | Includes online resources and index.
Identifiers: ISBN 9781532197444 (lib. bdg.) | ISBN 9781098270209 (ebook)
Subjects: LCSH: U.S. states--Juvenile literature. | Southwestern States--Juvenile literature. | Arizona--History--Juvenile literature. | Physical geography--United States--Juvenile literature.
Classification: DDC 979.1--dc23

Population demographics broken down by race and ethnicity come from the 2019 census estimate. Population totals come from the 2020 census.

CONTENTS

CHAPTER ONE

GRAND CANYON STATE

Tourists stand safely behind a railing and look out at the Grand Canyon. Steep cliff faces reach into the canyon. The walls are layered in reds and browns. The viewing platform the tourists stand on is more than 8,000 feet (2,440 m) above the canyon's bottom. When they squint, they can just make out the Colorado River rushing below. Over millions of years, the river created the canyon. Families take photos with the beautiful scenery. But it's hard to capture

Grand Canyon National Park has dozens of trails for people to hike on.

how impressive the canyon is. Arizona's nickname is the Grand Canyon state. Visitors can see why.

PETRIFIED FOREST

Today much of the northern region of Arizona is desert. But more than 200 million years ago, the area was forested. Volcanic eruptions and flooding destroyed the forest there. Some of the trees were swept underwater. They were quickly covered in thick layers of ash and other debris. Over time the wood from the trees became petrified. This means the wood was replaced by minerals. Some of these minerals came from the volcanic ash. Visitors to the Petrified Forest National Park can get a close look at the remains of the forest. The petrified wood there is Arizona's state fossil.

EXPLORING ARIZONA

Arizona is located in the southwestern United States. This region has mountain peaks and plateaus. Plateaus are flat, raised areas of land. The weather tends to be hot and dry. Arizona is famous for its deserts. But the state has forests too. Approximately 27 percent of the state is forested.

The Sonoran, *pictured*, Mojave, Chihuahuan, and Great Basin deserts are the four major North American deserts. All four cover parts of Arizona.

The Sonoran Desert is the largest desert in Arizona. It is in the southwestern region of the state. Parts of this desert receive fewer than 3 inches (7.6 cm) of rainfall a year. This is enough to sustain life for many different plants and animals. Sagebrush and other small bushes grow here. It is also home to saguaro (pronounced suh-WA-row) cacti and lizards called Gila (pronounced HEE-la) monsters. Saguaro cacti blossoms are Arizona's state flower. More than 350 bird species live in the Sonoran Desert. Coyotes and bobcats live there too.

PERSPECTIVES

ROGER NAYLOR

Tourism is an important part of Arizona's economy. Visitors spent more than $24 billion in the state in 2018. That year Roger Naylor was added to the Arizona Tourism Hall of Fame. He is a travel writer. He has written several books about must-see locations in Arizona. He says, "I want to leave Arizona a little better than I found it because . . . it's the great love of my life. I like to celebrate the people . . . or try to spread the word about what an amazing place we live in."

Arizona has several large cities in addition to its natural wonders. Tucson is one of the largest cities in Arizona. People first settled in the Tucson area more than 10,000 years ago. The Santa Cruz river flows through the city. Visitors today can see old churches and cultural museums.

Phoenix is Arizona's largest city. It is also the capital. Phoenix's central location in the state makes it a transportation hub. The heart of the city has historic buildings. The majority of Arizonans live in Phoenix and the surrounding cities. But each corner of the state offers something different.

MAP OF
ARIZONA

Arizona has many important cities and landmarks. What does the map show you about the locations of Arizona's cities? How does this map help you understand Arizona's geography?

CHAPTER TWO

HISTORY OF ARIZONA

Paleo-Indians were the earliest known peoples who lived in the Arizona region. Experts think they started living in the area approximately 13,500 years ago. This was during the Ice Age. The Paleo-Indians were nomadic. This means they followed herds of animals for food and moved often. At times, they hunted big game such as mammoths and mastodons.

Agriculture developed in Arizona approximately 4,000 years ago. People began

Throughout history, many people have visited the region of Arizona to see its remarkable sights.

The Hohokam material culture is known for red paint on light-colored pottery.

planting corn. These people continued to gather food such as cactus fruits from the land. But the development of agriculture allowed them to settle in villages. They built houses that could store corn.

Cultural differences started to develop between the peoples of Arizona. Historians today define these cultures based on the materials these peoples left behind. One example is the Hohokam material culture. Historians have found shell jewelry and pottery with red paint. Pit houses are another identifying feature of this culture. These are houses that were built into or around shallow pits. These people also dug the first irrigation canals in Arizona. These canals brought water from nearby rivers. They allowed people to settle farther from rivers and continue to grow crops.

Between approximately 1000 CE and 1500 CE, the Apache and Diné (Navajo) arrived in Arizona. They were hunter-gatherer peoples but began farming after arriving in the Southwest. These peoples took up the lifestyles of other American Indians in the area.

COLONIAL HISTORY

In 1539 Fray Marcos de Niza of Spain led an exploration in the Southwest in search of riches, such as gold. Other Spanish explorers came through the area shortly afterward. Not all of the Spanish who came to Arizona were seeking gold. Many were Christian missionaries. They tried to convert American Indians, such as the Akimel O'odham (Pima), to Christianity. The Spanish built settlements. They introduced livestock and crops, such as wheat, to the area. They also brought new diseases from Europe to the Arizona region, which killed many American Indians.

Eusebio Kino was a Jesuit missionary who came to southern Arizona in 1687. He established 24 missions, including San José de Tumacácori.

The Akimel O'odham formed uneasy alliances with the Spanish. The Spanish could help defend them against other American Indian nations. But the Spanish also forced their religion and culture on the Akimel O'odham. And they made the Akimel O'odham work in mines and on ranches. During the Akimel O'odham Revolt of 1751, the native people tried to push out the Spanish. The Spanish were able to reestablish control, but the revolt showed the frustration of the people. They were angry about the way the Spanish had treated them and their culture.

In 1810 the Mexican War of Independence (1810–1821) began. The former Spanish colony forced Spanish troops to leave the area. Eventually the Mexican government ousted all Spaniards, including missionaries. The Mexican-American War (1846–1848) followed. After Mexico was defeated, it gave most of modern-day Arizona to the United

GHOST TOWNS

Mining brought many people to Arizona. Towns centered around copper, silver, and gold mines. These towns thrived while mines were active. But economic troubles throughout the United States in the early 1900s caused many of the mines to shut down. Without work from the mines, people began leaving these towns. Some were completely abandoned. Today they are called ghost towns. People no longer live in the towns, but buildings from the mining era still stand. Tourists can visit these places. They can learn about the unique history and decline of each town.

States. The rest of Arizona became US territory with the Gadsden Purchase in 1854. The new US–Mexico border cut through the Tohono O'odham homeland, dividing the people between two countries.

The US government wanted to develop mines and railroads in Arizona. This would affect the lives of the American Indian peoples living in the region. The Apache tried to protect their land from the United States. This resulted in the Apache Wars (1861–1886), the longest conflict in US history. Nearly 25 percent of the US Army was based in the Southwest at the height of this war. At first the US Army wanted to kill all Apache people. They later forced all members of Apache nations to move to reservations. The Apache Wars ended in 1886, after the surrender of Apache leader Geronimo. The United States continued to expand into the region, and the territory's population grew quickly. People also arrived from other countries. Many Chinese workers came to Arizona and worked to build railroads.

STATEHOOD

On February 14, 1912, Arizona became the forty-eighth state. President Woodrow Wilson approved the creation of a national park to protect much of the Grand Canyon in 1919. Around this time, tourism in the state began increasing.

Arizona's population boomed in the 2000s. People moved from California and other US states in search of jobs. The 2020 Census showed Arizona was one of the fastest-growing states in the country.

PERSPECTIVES

SUPREME COURT JUSTICE

Sandra Day O'Connor grew up in Arizona. She started her career in the state Senate. Then, in 1981, she became the first woman on the US Supreme Court. "The power I exert on the court depends on the power of my arguments, not on my gender," she once said. O'Connor became known for careful research and decisions. O'Connor's votes on the Supreme Court helped settle legal questions about issues such as women's rights and election law. O'Connor retired from the Supreme Court in 2006.

ARIZONA
QUICK FACTS

Each US state has its own unique history and culture. How do Arizona's state symbols represent its culture? Did you find any of these symbols surprising?

Abbreviation: AZ
Nickname: The Grand Canyon State
Motto: *Ditat Deus* (God enriches)
Date of statehood: February 14, 1912
Capital: Phoenix
Population: 7,278,717
Area: 113,990 square miles (295,233 sq km)

STATE SYMBOLS

State bird
Cactus wren

State metal
Copper

State flower
Saguaro cactus blossom

State tree
Palo verde

Today Arizona's government has three branches. The executive branch is led by a governor. The legislative branch makes laws. It is made up of two groups, the House of Representatives and the Senate. The judicial branch is the court system.

The US government recognizes 22 American Indian nations in Arizona. Some American Indians live on reservations that have separate governments. But they also participate in state and federal politics.

FURTHER EVIDENCE

Chapter Two describes some of the American Indian peoples that are part of Arizona's history and culture. What was one of the main points of this chapter? What evidence is included to support this point? Read the article at the website below. Does the information on the website support the information from the chapter? Does it present new evidence?

HISTORY

abdocorelibrary.com/arizona

CHAPTER THREE

GEOGRAPHY AND CLIMATE

Arizona has mountains and canyons. Many of the state's rocky features come from ancient volcanoes. These volcanoes also gave rise to important minerals, such as copper, found in Arizona. The northern and eastern areas of the state are part of the Colorado Plateau. This is high, rugged, flat land. The Painted Desert is found here. This desert is made of red, purple, pink, and yellow rocky hills. The state's highest point is Humphreys Peak. It is located in the

The Painted Desert covers more than 93,500 acres (37,838 ha).

north-central region. The mountains there are forested. The trees that grow there, such as the ponderosa pine, must be able to survive on high ground. Animals such as black bears and deer live in this mountain region.

The middle of the state is the transition zone. This region has rolling hills. Its elevation is slightly lower than the north and higher than the south. Grasses grow on these plains and hilly areas. Coyotes, jackrabbits, foxes, turkeys, quail, rattlesnakes, and scorpions can be found here. They also live throughout the state.

Approximately half of Arizona's land is desert. Human-made lakes in desert regions store water for people and wildlife. The desert environment is challenging for animals. But some plants and animals have adapted to survive there. Diamondback rattlesnakes spend the hottest parts of the day in the shade of shrubs. Javelinas, which look like wild boar, feed on desert plants. The cactus wren is the state

Saguaros are protected by Arizona law. Cutting down or damaging saguaros without a permit can result in fines and criminal charges.

bird of Arizona. It nests in cacti year-round, where it is protected from predators.

Cacti, such as the saguaro cactus, grow throughout the state. Their thick skins prevent them from losing water in the desert heat. Cactus skin also expands to help store water. Arizona's state tree, the palo verde, is another desert plant. It can be found in the Sonoran Desert. It has deep roots that help it survive droughts and flash floods, both of which are common in the desert.

LARGEST US CACTUS

The saguaro cactus is the largest cactus in North America. It grows up to 50 feet (15 m) tall. But surviving in the desert is not easy. One way the saguaro survives is by growing very slowly. It can take 20 to 50 years for a saguaro to reach 3 feet (0.9 m) tall. The saguaro cactus only grows in the Sonoran Desert, which covers southern Arizona and western Sonora, Mexico. A few saguaros grow near the border of the Sonoran Desert in southeastern California too.

HOT AND DRY

Overall, Arizona's weather is very warm and dry. Some parts of the state get more than 300 days of sunshine per year. Some regions receive only approximately 8 inches (20 cm) of rainfall each year. The dry weather puts Arizona at risk for dust storms. Dust clouds can be thousands of feet high and travel multiple miles. Dust lingers in the air after these storms. Breathing in dusty air can cause health problems. Dust storms also hurt plants, including crops.

Other areas of the state receive significant amounts of snowfall. Flagstaff receives an average of 102 inches

People in Arizona can enjoy winter activities, such as cross-country skiing and snowboarding, in the mountains.

(259 cm) of snow each year. Snow is also common in other mountainous areas of the state.

Climate change is a threat to Arizona. Hotter temperatures cause water to evaporate quickly in the summer months. If rivers and lakes dry out, animals must travel farther to find water. People depend on rivers such as the Gila River, Salt River, and Verde River for water. And many people would suffer if the Colorado River dried up. That river is responsible for

PERSPECTIVES

HOPI AND CLIMATE CHANGE

The Hopi people have planted corn in the Arizona region for more than 2,000 years. In 2020 Arizona experienced one of its worst droughts in history. Many crops did not survive. Climate change has brought increasingly dry weather to the area. Beatrice Norton is a member of the Hopi Tribe. She has seen corn harvests become smaller due to climate change. She said, "We are dependent on this corn for our ceremonies, our way of life, to be complete. . . . Sooner or later we're going to be missing a big piece of what is a part of our life as Hopi."

providing water to 40 million people in seven states, including Arizona. The Colorado River gets water from snowmelt on the Rocky Mountains. But warmer temperatures mean less snowfall. Rivers and lakes that depend on snowmelt have lower water levels as climate change continues.

Climate change also makes the threat of wildfires worse. Hotter and drier land has a greater risk of catching fire. Plants such as dry grasses can quickly ignite and spread the flames.

STRAIGHT TO THE SOURCE

Mary Kidder Rak was an author and rancher who lived in southern Arizona in the early to mid-1900s. She wrote about her life on the ranch and the beauty of Arizona:

> *When we want to hear our visitors say "Oh!" and "Ah!" we take them to a little knoll back of our house and show them the mountains that rise on either side of Red Rock Canyon, crimsoned and glorified by the long rays of the setting sun. Glowing with reflected fire, the rocks stand out against the purple of more distant peaks and the pale azure of the evening sky. The canyon . . . [ends] on smooth hills matted with the pine needles of centuries.*

Source: Mary Kidder Rak. "A Cowman's Wife." *Hathi Trust*, 1934, p. 92, babel.hathitrust.org. Accessed 11 Mar. 2021.

WHAT'S THE BIG IDEA

Take a close look at this passage. What is the main connection being made between Arizona and its landscape? What reactions does Rak expect from her visitors?

CHAPTER FOUR

RESOURCES AND ECONOMY

Four important resources shaped Arizona's economy through the early 1900s. They were citrus, cotton, cattle, and copper. They are sometimes referred to as the four C's. Parts of Arizona's economy is influenced by a fifth *C*, climate. The climate affects agriculture.

Citrus production increased as irrigation systems were built. Cotton boomed in the 1910s. It was used in many products, including clothing. In 1918 about 1.75 million cattle were

There are thousands of cattle ranches and farms in Arizona.

Pima is a type of cotton grown in Arizona. It helps create soft, strong fabrics.

raised in Arizona. This provided beef to the country. Arizona's copper mines were especially important for the United States during World War I (1914–1918). Nearly 40 percent of US copper came from the state. It was used in wiring and weapon casings.

INDUSTRIES TODAY

Mining remains an important part of Arizona's economy. Arizona is the top copper-producing state. This metal is used to make wires and coins. Other materials are mined within Arizona too. Coal is found in northeastern reservations. It is commonly used for fuel. Uranium is a metal that is mined for nuclear energy.

Arizona has a long growing season, which is useful for agriculture. Cattle, sheep, and hogs are raised in Arizona. They provide food for the United States and other countries. Arizona continues to be one of the leading cotton producers in the country. And the state is still known for citrus crops such as lemons, limes, and grapefruits. People in Arizona also grow grapes, nuts, and grains.

Manufacturing and tourism are the biggest parts of Arizona's economy.

PERSPECTIVES

FARMING AND WATER STRESS

Arizona farmers depend on the Colorado River to grow crops. But droughts have put stress on the water system. In 2019 Arizona received a reduced share of the Colorado River water supply because of droughts. This put strain on farms. Selwyn Justice is an Arizona citrus farmer. He works with the University of Arizona to develop technology that will help farmers grow crops during droughts. But scientists expect droughts to get worse. Justice says, "There are some places in Arizona that inevitably are going to have to stop farming."

WINTER TOURISTS

Some people live in Arizona during only the winter months. They come to Arizona to escape harsh winters in colder areas of the country. These people are known as snowbirds. There are fewer than 4,000 people who live in Quartzsite, Arizona, year-round. But in the winter of 2017, more than 2 million snowbirds and other travelers visited the town.

The state makes electronics, aluminum, and communication products. Tourism is increasing. Arizona is known for its scenic landscapes. Some of these places are preserved in the state's three national parks and four national monuments. Arizona also has other historical sites that are protected by the US government. Many people come to visit these places.

Arizona's warm climate attracts people to the state. For example, many major league baseball teams have spring training practices in Arizona. The teams that play there make up the Cactus League. Additionally,

The Chicago Cubs are part of the Cactus League.

a number of people retire to Arizona. People move to the state when they finish their careers. They find the weather and scenery relaxing.

EXPLORE ONLINE

Chapter Four describes the various parts of Arizona's economy. As you know, every source is different. How is the information from the website the same as the information in Chapter Four? What new information did you learn from the website?

ARIZONA'S FIVE C'S ARE: COPPER, CATTLE, COTTON, CITRUS AND CLIMATE

abdocorelibrary.com/arizona

CHAPTER FIVE

PEOPLE AND PLACES

Arizona is home to more than 7 million people. Arizona has one of the fastest-growing populations in the country. In 2021 Phoenix was named the fastest-growing city in the United States for the fifth year in a row. The majority of Arizona's population is concentrated in its cities. Approximately 60 percent of the state's population lives in Maricopa County, where Phoenix is located.

More than 1.6 million people live in Phoenix.

Mexican food is found throughout the state.

White people who are not Hispanic or Latino make up 54 percent of Arizona's population. Approximately 5 percent of Arizonans are Black and 4 percent are Asian. Approximately 32 percent of Arizona's population is Hispanic or Latino. The vast majority of Arizona's Hispanic population has Mexican ancestry. This is because Arizona was historically part of Mexico. Mexican culture is part of Arizona's art, food, music, and other traditions. The Arizona Hispanic Chamber of Commerce supports and promotes Hispanic-owned businesses. The Arizona Latino Arts & Cultural Center supports local artists in Phoenix. In 2020 the Phoenix City Council unanimously approved plans to build a

Latino Cultural Center in the city. The center will host events, workshops, exhibits, and more to celebrate Hispanic and Latino cultures in Arizona. Festivals around the state allow people to celebrate Hispanic and Latino cultures.

Many Latin American immigrants come to Arizona due to its location on the US–Mexico border. Immigrants are people who come to the United States from other countries. Many

PERSPECTIVES

INTERNATIONAL SONORAN DESERT ALLIANCE

Ajo, Arizona, is a historic mining town. Mining operations shut down in the mid-1980s. The town's economy has struggled since then. The International Sonoran Desert Alliance is located in Ajo. The organization focuses on creative reuse. It wants to transform Ajo into an arts town. It works to bring artists and art events into the area. Tracy Taft is a former director of the organization. She said, "We're creating something that Ajo needs badly. Ajo's only hope for becoming really a flourishing town again is that kind of niche [specialized] tourism."

ANNIE DODGE WAUNEKA

Annie Dodge Wauneka was a member of the Navajo Nation. She was born in 1910. She survived the Spanish flu. This was a deadly disease that killed more than 50 million people worldwide. Then she became a health activist. Wauneka was one of first women on the Navajo Nation Tribal Council. She created an English–Diné Bizaad dictionary to help Diné people communicate with doctors. In 1963 she received the Presidential Medal of Freedom for her work. She died in 1997.

people immigrate to the United States legally. But some cross the border without the proper legal documents that allow them to live in the United States. An estimated 4 percent of Arizona's population is undocumented.

American Indian people make up approximately 5 percent of Arizona's population. There are 20 American Indian reservations throughout the state. The Navajo Nation is the largest reservation in the United States. It extends from Arizona into New Mexico and Utah and has a population of more than 250,000.

Festivals such as the Navajo Nation Fair are opportunities for Arizona's American Indian peoples to celebrate their foods, arts, traditions, and more.

Influences from American Indian cultures are widespread. American Indian craftspeople make pottery and jewelry. Many American Indian communities raise awareness about their cultures at the Arizona Indian Festival. Each nation celebrates its own unique culture through arts and foods.

Many celebrities have grown up in Arizona. Academy Award–winning actress Emma Stone was born in Scottsdale. Professional baseball player Cody Bellinger was also born in Scottsdale.

IMPORTANT PLACES

Tucson, Sedona, and Scottsdale have large artist communities. Phoenix is a big music center. Orchestras, ballet, and theaters are mainly found in the state's central region.

Arizona has many natural attractions. The Grand Canyon and Petrified Forest are popular national parks. Both have colorful rock features. Meteor Crater is a hole that is 1 mile (1.6 km) wide and 550 feet (168 m) deep. It formed 50,000 years ago when a meteor from space struck Earth. Arizona often attracts visitors for outdoor activities. These include hiking, camping, photography, and seeing historical sites. Visitors can also enjoy skiing in Arizona's mountains.

In Arizona, tourists are able to learn about the Hispanic and American Indian cultures that shaped the state's history. Visitors can enjoy dry, sunny weather even during the middle of winter. Arizona has memorable features that make it a unique state.

STRAIGHT TO THE SOURCE

National Hispanic American Heritage Month takes place every year from September 15 to October 15. In 2019 Arizona governor Doug Ducey issued a statement recognizing the event:

> *Hispanic Heritage Month celebrates the accomplishments of Arizonans of Hispanic heritage—whose cultural, economic, and civic contributions have made Arizona the thriving and vibrant place it is today. . . . From our history to our people, Hispanic heritage is woven into the fabric of our state, creating a richness and diversity today that's uniquely and undeniably Arizonan. All this month, we are proud to honor the pivotal role those of Hispanic descent have played in shaping Arizona as a place of opportunity for all.*

Source: Doug Ducey. "Arizona Celebrates Hispanic Heritage Month." *Office of the Governor Doug Ducey*, 16 Sept. 2019, azgovernor.gov. Accessed 15 Sept. 2021.

CONSIDER YOUR AUDIENCE

Adapt this passage for a different audience, such as your principal or friends. Write a blog post conveying this same information for the new audience. How does your post differ from the original text and why?

IMPORTANT DATES

13,500 years ago
People first live in the Arizona area.

1539
Fray Marcos de Niza leads the first Spanish expedition that covers present-day Arizona.

1751
The Akimel O'odham revolt against the Spanish.

1854
The United States purchases southern Arizona from Mexico in the Gadsden Purchase.

1861
A conflict known as the Apache Wars begins between the US government and the Apache peoples. It ends in 1886.

1912
Arizona becomes the forty-eighth US state on February 14.

1919
Grand Canyon National Park is founded.

1963
Annie Dodge Wauneka wins the Presidential Medal of Freedom for her work as a health-care activist.

1981
Sandra Day O'Connor becomes the first female US Supreme Court justice.

STOP AND THINK

Surprise Me

Chapter Four discusses important resources that are part of Arizona's economy. After reading this book, what two or three facts about Arizona's economy did you find most surprising? Write a few sentences about each fact. Why did you find each fact surprising?

Why Do I Care?

Maybe you have not visited the Grand Canyon. But that doesn't mean you can't think about its importance. Why is it important to protect areas of land? How did the Grand Canyon affect the lives of people in Arizona throughout history, and how does it affect people today?

You Are There

This book discusses several of Arizona's impressive landforms. Imagine you are traveling through the state. Write a letter home telling your friends what you see. What do you notice about the landscape? Be sure to add plenty of detail to your notes.

Another View

This book talks about climate change in Arizona. As you know, every source is different. Ask a librarian or another adult to help you find another source about this topic. Write a short essay comparing and contrasting the new source's point of view with that of this book's author. What is the point of view of each author? How are they similar and why? How are they different and why?

GLOSSARY

activist
a person who takes action to make social or political changes

ancestry
a person's family members from the past

canal
a long, human-made ditch that allows water to flow from one area to another

elevation
the height above sea level

evaporate
to change from a liquid to a gas

irrigation
the process of watering crops though human-made means, such as pipes

missionary
a person who is working for a religious goal, usually to spread his or her faith

nuclear
relating to the type of energy produced by splitting atoms; commonly associated with atomic bombs

reservation
an area of land set aside for American Indian people

ONLINE RESOURCES

To learn more about Arizona, visit our free resource websites below.

Core Library CONNECTION
FREE! COMMON CORE MULTIMEDIA RESOURCES

Visit **abdocorelibrary.com** or scan this QR code for free Common Core resources for teachers and students, including vetted activities, multimedia, and booklinks, for deeper subject comprehension.

Booklinks NONFICTION NETWORK
FREE! ONLINE NONFICTION RESOURCES

Visit **abdobooklinks.com** or scan this QR code for free additional online weblinks for further learning. These links are routinely monitored and updated to provide the most current information available.

LEARN MORE

Bell, Samantha S. *Traditional Stories of the Southwest Nations.* Abdo, 2018.

Durrie, Karen. *Arizona.* Weigl, 2019.

INDEX

About the Author

Audrey Harrison lives in Minnesota. She enjoys mystery novels and jigsaw puzzles. She has visited 32 states and counting.